7.60   J 978

REAL-LIFE
SCIENTIFIC
ADVENTURES

LEWIS AND CLARK EXPLORE THE LOUISIANA TERRITORY

RACHAEL MORLOCK

PowerKiDS press™

New York

Published in 2019 by The Rosen Publishing Group, Inc.
29 East 21st Street, New York, NY 10010

First Edition

Editor: Theresa Morlock
Book Design: Reann Nye

Photo Credits: Cover, p. 1 David David Gallery/SuperStock/Getty Images; p. 4 https://en.wikipedia.org/wiki/File:Official_Presidential_portrait_of_Thomas_Jefferson_(by_Rembrandt_Peale,_1800).jpg; p. 5 Ad_hominem/Shutterstock.com; p. 6 Florilegius/SSPL/Getty Images; p. 7 (Lewis) https://commons.wikimedia.org/wiki/File:Meriweather_Lewis-Charles_Willson_Peale.jpg; p. 7 (Clark) https://en.wikipedia.org/wiki/File:William_Clark-Charles_Willson_Peale.jpg; p. 9 (top) https://commons.wikimedia.org/wiki/File:American_Philosophical_Society_(20864173941).jpg; pp. 9 (bottom), 10, 29 (top) Courtesy of the Library of Congress; p. 11 (top) Ed Vebell/Archive Photos/Getty Images; p. 11 (bottom) kavram/Shutterstock.com; p. 13 Andrew B Hall/Shutterstock.com; p. 14 ESB Professional/Shutterstock.com; p. 15 https://commons.wikimedia.org/wiki/File:Clark_Family_Collection-_Volume_4._Voorhis_Journal_No._4,_page_5,_October_22-28,_1806.jpg; p. 16 Henk Bentlage/Shutterstock.com; p. 17 (top) NaturesMomentsuk/Shutterstock.com; p. 17 (bottom) sergioboccardo/Shutterstock.com; p. 18 Everett Historical/Shutterstock.com; p. 19 SuperStock/Getty Images; p. 21 Ace Diamond/Shutterstock.com; p. 23 (top) https://commons.wikimedia.org/wiki/File:Lewis_and_clark-expedition.jpg; p. 23 (bottom) Martha Marks/Shutterstock.com; p. 24 Nagel Photography/Shutterstock.com; p. 25 Bob Pool/Photographer's Choice/Getty Images; p. 27 (top) https://commons.wikimedia.org/wiki/File:Pompeys_Pillar_NM_(9424545304).jpg; p. 27 (bottom) Katherine Welles/Shutterstock.com; p. 28 https://commons.wikimedia.org/wiki/File:Detail_Lewis_%26_Clark_at_Three_Forks.jpg; p. 29 (bottom) Jean-Erick PASQUIER/Gamma-Rapho/Getty Images.

Library of Congress Cataloging-in-Publication Data

Names: Morlock, Rachael, author.
Title: Lewis and Clark explore the Louisiana Territory / Rachael Morlock.
Description: New York : PowerKids Press, 2019. | Series: Real-life scientific
  adventures | Includes index.
Identifiers: LCCN 2017054527| ISBN 9781508168508 (library bound) | ISBN
  9781508168522 (pbk.) | ISBN 9781508168539 (6 pack)
Subjects: LCSH: Lewis and Clark Expedition (1804-1806)–Juvenile literature.
  | Lewis, Meriwether, 1774-1809–Juvenile literature. | Clark, William,
  1770-1838–Juvenile literature. | West (U.S.)–Discovery and
  exploration–Juvenile literature.
Classification: LCC F592.7 .M678 2018 | DDC 917.804/2–dc23
LC record available at https://lccn.loc.gov/2017054527

Manufactured in the United States of America

CPSIA Compliance Information: Batch #CS18PK: For Further Information contact Rosen Publishing, New York, New York at 1-800-237-9932

CONTENTS

A GROWING NATION 4

LEWIS AND CLARK 6

PREPARING FOR THE JOURNEY 8

TO THE WEST! 10

THE CORPS OF DISCOVERY 12

MAPPING THE TERRITORY 14

SCIENTIFIC INVESTIGATION 16

AMERICAN INDIANS 18

SACAGAWEA 20

LIFE ON THE TRAIL 22

THE MIGHTY PACIFIC 24

ON THE WAY HOME 26

THE VOYAGE OF DISCOVERY 28

GLOSSARY 31

INDEX 32

WEBSITES 32

A GROWING NATION

When Thomas Jefferson became president in 1801, most Americans lived within 50 miles of the Atlantic Ocean. The land west of the Mississippi River was not yet part of the United States. Although American Indians had lived in the West for centuries, few white Americans or Europeans had explored this part of North America.

Jefferson hoped to expand the United States so it would stretch from the Atlantic to the Pacific Ocean. He seized an important opportunity to nearly double the property owned by the United States through the Louisiana Purchase. In 1803, for $15 million, the United States bought a vast area of land from France. Even before it became part of the United States, Jefferson was planning an expedition across the Louisiana Territory.

Thomas Jefferson

4

The Louisiana Territory was the homeland of many American Indians. French fur traders and trappers also traveled through this area, but much of it was unmapped and unfamiliar to white Americans.

LEWIS AND CLARK

The expedition Jefferson was planning had three main purposes. First, it would scientifically **document** the plants, animals, and **resources** of the West. Second, it would gather information about American Indian tribes and make positive connections with their leaders. Third, the expedition would try to find the easiest path across the continent by traveling along waterways.

Jefferson knew that only a strong person with many talents could successfully lead the expedition. They needed

EXPEDITION REPORT

Record keeping was important on the expedition. Lewis and Clark kept journals to report on their travels and the new people, plants, animals, and settings they **encountered**. Much of the historical information available about their explorations comes from these journals.

Lewis and Clark first met in the U.S. Army in Ohio. Their different personalities and abilities worked together to make them strong team members, leaders, and lifelong friends.

William Clark

Meriwether Lewis

to be **dedicated**, inventive, scientific, and **diplomatic**. Jefferson saw all these qualities in his secretary, Meriwether Lewis. Lewis was eager to join the expedition. He wrote a letter to his friend William Clark asking him to work by his side as a captain. Lewis and Clark were ready to establish a path across America.

PREPARING FOR THE JOURNEY

Lewis had already learned a great deal about how to study animals, press plants, observe the stars, and **navigate** from Jefferson and others. In order to learn more, Lewis went to Philadelphia, Pennsylvania, to talk with experts in science, mapmaking, **botany**, medicine, and languages.

In addition to polishing their skills, Lewis and Clark also needed to buy and organize supplies, **recruit** members, and learn as much as possible about the land and people of the West. Clark set up a training camp on the edge of the Louisiana Territory for the new members of the expedition. Meanwhile, Lewis went to Saint Louis, Missouri, to gather information and study the few existing maps of the Missouri River. On May 14, 1804, the members of the expedition left their camp to explore the Louisiana Territory.

The American Philosophical Society in Philadelphia was a perfect training ground for Lewis. Today, visitors can view the Lewis and Clark journals and scientific **specimens** that are housed there.

This letter from Jefferson provided Lewis with instructions as he prepared for the expedition.

TO THE WEST!

Travel along the Missouri River was challenging. A large keelboat had been made especially for the expedition. It was 55 feet (16.8 m) long, with room for about 20

replica of Lewis and Clark's keelboat

men to row and more space for supplies. Depending on the conditions of the river, the men could row, raise the sail, use long poles to push the boat through the water, or pull the boat with ropes. They traveled about 10 to 15 miles (16.1 to 24.1 km) a day on the keelboat and two smaller boats called pirogues.

The expedition planned to follow the Missouri River as far as possible. From there, the men would leave the water to cross the Rocky Mountains. On the other side, they hoped to quickly find and follow the Columbia River to the Pacific Ocean.

Lewis and Clark hoped to find the Northwest Passage, a water route across the continent. They counted on information from Indians and trappers to learn about rivers like the Missouri.

Missouri River

THE CORPS OF DISCOVERY

The expedition company was called the Corps of Discovery. Lewis and Clark were careful to recruit young, healthy, unmarried men who were prepared for hard work, dangerous conditions, and a long separation from their families. The youngest member of the Corps was 17 and the oldest was 35.

In addition to soldiers, the Corps also included **interpreters**. George Drouillard was the son of a French Canadian and a Shawnee Indian. As an interpreter, he mainly used sign language to communicate with Indians they met along the way. Drouillard was one of 33 members who completed the entire expedition. Only one life was lost on the journey. Sergeant Charles Floyd died, probably from a burst **appendix**, on August 20, 1804.

EXPEDITION REPORT

The expedition included York, a black man kept as a slave by Clark. He faced the journey's hardships with the others, but returned to life as a slave at the end. For the Indians they encountered, York inspired awe and surprise.

Floyd was buried at Floyd's Bluff. The Corps members stopped there to honor him. Today, a monument stands on the bluff, or hill, in Floyd's memory.

MAPPING THE TERRITORY

When the expedition began, little was known about the **geography** of the Northwest. The Missouri River was documented as far as the villages of the Mandan people

in present-day North Dakota. There were also reports from explorers who entered the Columbia River from the Pacific Ocean. The layout of rivers, mountains, and other features in the area in between was a blank that Lewis and Clark intended to fill in.

Clark had experience as a cartographer, or mapmaker, in the army. He used those skills to keep careful geographical records of the Corps' journey and surrounding land. Clark often questioned the Indians and trappers they met about geography. Before mapping an area, he would check with several people to be sure his information was correct.

Clark used drawings and notes from his journals to create detailed maps of the expedition. He named rivers and other features after expedition members, friends, and important events or experiences.

SCIENTIFIC INVESTIGATION

While Clark made maps, Lewis recorded information about plants, animals, weather, and the natural resources the Corps came across. He collected seeds and sketched, pressed, and described the plants of the West.

In his journals, Lewis noted unfamiliar animals the party met. He described grizzly bears, bison, prairie dogs, pronghorn antelopes, mountain goats, and coyotes. He collected skins, skeletons, and even live animals.

Lewis and Clark sent the keelboat back along the Missouri River the next spring. They loaded it with their maps, reports, Indian objects, and scientific specimens. The shipment would make its way to Jefferson with news of the expedition.

prairie dogs

Pronghorn antelopes were described by Lewis, who also sent their skeletons to Jefferson.

American bison

AMERICAN INDIANS

One of the expedition's goals was to make friendly connections with American Indian tribes of the West. Jefferson wanted to learn more about the American Indians, including their numbers, traditions, and more. He also wanted to create positive relationships that would encourage Indians to trade with the United States instead of foreigners.

Lewis and Clark greeted each tribe with a special ceremony. They made speeches and gave gifts that were symbols of peace, but they also announced the strength

This Thomas Jefferson Indian Peace Medal was made in 1801.

This painting illustrates Lewis's first meeting with Shoshoni Indians. The party always carried items to give or trade. Beads, handkerchiefs, and Jefferson's peace medals were offered as gifts to Indians.

and wealth of the United States. Indian chiefs were presented with documents and medals that backed the idea of Jefferson as their chief and president. At the same time, the men of the expedition depended on the Indians for information, food, and safe passage across the country.

SACAGAWEA

In the fall of 1804, the Corps arrived at the villages of the Mandan people. They built a fort and spent the winter assembling reports, getting to know their Hidatsa and Mandan neighbors, and preparing for the journey ahead.

That winter, Toussaint Charbonneau introduced himself and his Shoshoni wife, Sacagawea, to Lewis and Clark. The captains knew they would soon need to trade with Shoshoni Indians for horses to cross the Rocky Mountains. The couple joined the party as interpreters. Just 17 years old and a new mother, Sacagawea made key contributions to the voyage. She shared her knowledge of plants and recognized important landmarks. Perhaps most importantly, the presence of a mother and child demonstrated the party's peaceful nature to the Indians they met.

EXPEDITION REPORT

Communicating with the Shoshoni Indians required many languages. The Shoshoni spoke to Sacagawea, who translated their words into Hidatsa for Charbonneau. Charbonneau spoke French to a member of the Corps, who delivered the message in English to Lewis and Clark.

Sacagawea traveled on foot, on horseback, and in canoes while carrying her infant son, Jean Baptiste. The baby was called "Little Pomp" or "Pompey" by the members of the expedition.

LIFE ON THE TRAIL

After leaving the Mandan villages, the Corps reached the Missouri River's limits and soon began crossing the Rocky Mountains on Shoshoni horses. Throughout the expedition, the crew had suffered from severe weather, mosquitoes, illnesses, and the dangers of wild animals. Now, they also faced hungry days on a snowy path through seemingly endless mountains.

The men had eaten up to nine pounds of meat a day when hunting parties supplied bison, elk, bear, and beaver meat. In contrast, food in the mountains was scarce and the party had to eat some of the horses. After crossing the Rockies, the men traded with the Nez Perce Indians they met for roots, dried fish, and dogs for their meals. They crafted canoes and continued west toward the Pacific Ocean on the Clearwater River.

EXPEDITION REPORT

Lewis was accompanied throughout the expedition by his black Newfoundland dog, Seaman. An excellent hunter and watchdog, Seaman also tackled many dangers of the journey. He was troubled by mosquitoes, marched over painful prickly pear, and scuffled with wild animals.

Lewis and Clark left the Louisiana Territory to continue to the Pacific Ocean. From the Clearwater River, they followed the Snake River to the Columbia River and met many Indian tribes.

Snake River, Idaho

THE MIGHTY PACIFIC

Crossing the mountains had taken much longer than expected. The Corps members had little time to waste if they were to reach the Pacific Ocean before winter. Unfortunately, the Columbia River was marked by challenges. Rapids and storms made the waters rough and choppy. Fleas bothered the crew, their clothes rotted in the damp and rainy conditions, and the Indians they met asked high prices for food and goods. In November 1805, the Corps finally reached the Pacific Ocean.

EXPEDITION REPORT

The corps built a winter camp on the southern bank of the Columbia River and named it Fort Clatsop after the neighboring Indian tribe. Elk provided meat and skins that the men used to make clothes and moccasins for the return journey.

Cape Disappointment lies at the northern side of the Columbia River where it meets the Pacific Ocean. The Corps first viewed the ocean and explored the coast from this spot.

The expedition would remain near the ocean for the winter, but they needed to build a camp. The captains made an unusual choice to decide as a group and vote on the location. Every member of the expedition, including York and Sacagawea, cast an equal vote.

ON THE WAY HOME

The Corps had completed its mission to travel across America to the Pacific Ocean. During its final winter, Clark worked on his maps, Lewis recorded scientific reports, and the men prepared supplies for the return journey. They left Fort Clatsop in March to retrace their travels, this time heading east.

After crossing the Rocky Mountains once more, the Corps divided to follow different routes and gain more geographical information. When they met again, they moved quickly along the Missouri River. The expedition said goodbye to Sacagawea's family at the Mandan villages. Travel downriver was fast, and the Corps arrived at Saint Louis on September 23, 1806. After two-and-a-half years and more than 8,000 miles of travel, they were greeted with lively celebrations.

Clark named this monumental rock formation Pompey's Tower after Sacagawea's son. It's now known as Pompey's Pillar. The date and signature Clark carved into the rock are still visible.

THE VOYAGE OF DISCOVERY

Lewis and Clark hoped to discover a route of rivers for traveling across the continent. Instead, land travel was required for the full westward journey. Lengthy **portages** and the huge extent of the Rocky Mountain range ruled out the possibility of a Northwest Passage by water.

In every other sense, their expedition was a success. They studied the people, plants, animals, and geography of the Louisiana Territory and more with attention and detail. They made peaceful connections with Indian tribes and opened new trade opportunities. Their journey was an important first step in the expansion of the United States from the Atlantic to the Pacific. The daring adventures of the Corps of Discovery raised a new curiosity about life in the West that would inspire generations of Americans.

Clark's carefully mapped observations offered an image of western geography that was much different from the landscape the Corps expected to explore. The maps became a guide for others heading West.

White Cliffs, Montana

Into the West

March 4, 1801

Thomas Jefferson becomes the third president of the United States.

July 4, 1803

The Louisiana Purchase is announced. The purchase doubles the size of the United States territory.

March 10, 1804

Lewis and Clark are present at a ceremony in Saint Louis officially transferring the Louisiana Territory from France to the United States.

August 20, 1804

Sergeant Charles Floyd dies and is buried at Floyd's Bluff.

November 4, 1804

Sacagawea and Toussaint Charbonneau join the expedition as interpreters.

February 11, 1805

Sacagawea gives birth to Jean Baptiste.

April 7, 1805

The keelboat is sent back to Saint Louis. The remaining 33 members of the expedition continue west.

August 12, 1805

The shipment of reports, maps, specimens, and Indian items sent on the keelboat reaches the East.

August 31, 1805

The Corps begins to cross the Rocky Mountains through the Bitterroot Range.

October 16, 1805

The Corps begins its journey on the Columbia River.

November 1805

The Corps of Discovery reaches the Pacific Ocean.

January 4, 1806

Jefferson meets with a group of Indian chiefs who had encountered Lewis and Clark the previous year.

March 23, 1806

The Corps leaves Fort Clatsop and begins the return journey.

August 14, 1806

The expedition returns to the Mandan villages and parts with Sacagawea, Charbonneau, and Jean Baptiste.

September 23, 1806

The Corps of Discovery arrives in Saint Louis at the end of the expedition.

GLOSSARY

appendix: A body part attached to the lower end of the large intestine.

botany: The study of plant life.

dedicated: Devoted to a purpose or cause.

diplomatic: Skilled at dealing with other people or nations.

document: To record information about or descriptions of something. Also, a formal piece of writing.

encounter: To meet.

geography: The natural parts and features of an area of land.

interpreter: Someone who translates for speakers of different languages.

navigate: To find one's way over water or land.

portage: The carrying of boats or goods on land from one body of water to another.

recruit: To enlist or hire new members.

resource: A usable supply of something.

specimen: A scientific sample.

INDEX

A

American Indians, 4, 5, 6, 11, 12, 14, 16, 18, 19, 20, 22, 23, 24, 28, 30
American Philosophical Society, 9
Atlantic Ocean, 4, 28

C

Cape Disappointment, 25
Charbonneau, Toussaint, 20, 30
Clearwater River, 22, 23
Columbia River, 10, 14, 23, 24, 25, 30
Corps of Discovery, 12, 13, 14, 16, 20, 22, 24, 25, 26, 28, 29, 30

D

Drouillard, George, 12

F

Floyd, Charles, 12, 13, 30
Fort Clatsop, 24, 30
France, 4, 30

H

Hidatsa, 20

I

Idaho, 23

J

Jean Baptiste, 21, 30
Jefferson, Thomas, 4, 6, 8, 9, 16, 17, 18, 19, 30

M

Mandan people, 14, 20, 22, 26, 30
Mississippi River, 4, 16
Missouri, 8
Missouri River, 8, 10, 11, 14, 22, 26
Montana, 29

N

Nez Perce Indians, 22
North America, 4
North Dakota, 14
Northwest Passage, 11, 28

P

Pacific Ocean, 4, 10, 14, 22, 24, 25, 26, 28, 30
Pennsylvania, 8
Philadelphia, 8, 9

R

Rocky Mountains, 10, 20, 22, 26, 28, 30

S

Sacagawea, 20, 21, 25, 26, 27, 30
Saint Louis, 8, 26, 30
Seaman, 22
Shoshoni people, 19, 20
Snake River, 23

U

United States, 4, 5, 18, 19, 28, 30

Y

York, 12, 25

WEBSITES

Due to the changing nature of Internet links, PowerKids Press has developed an online list of websites related to the subject of this book. This site is updated regularly. Please use this link to access the list: www.powerkidslinks.com/rlsa/louisi